cushions & covers

an easy-to-make project book

How to sew and embellish 20 gorgeous bolsters, pillows and slipcovers.
Simple-to-follow techniques shown in 200 photographs

EMMA CLEGG

LORENZ BOOKS

This edition is published by Lorenz Books,
an imprint of Anness Publishing Ltd,
Blaby Road, Wigston, Leicestershire
LE18 4SE; info@anness.com

www.lorenzbooks.com; www.annesspublishing.com

If you like the images in this book and would like to
investigate using them for publishing, promotions or
advertising, please visit our website
www.practicalpictures.com for more information.

Publisher: Joanna Lorenz
Editorial Director: Helen Sudell
Project Editors: Emma Clegg
   and Zoë Hughes-Gough
Designer: Adelle Morris
Production Controller: Helen Wang

© Anness Publishing Ltd 2012

A CIP catalogue record for this book is available from
the British Library.

Previously published as *Creating Cushions
& Cushion Covers*

PUBLISHER'S NOTE
Although the advice and information in this book are
believed to be accurate and true at the time of going to
press, neither the authors nor the publisher can accept
any legal responsibility or liability for any errors or
omissions that may have been made nor for any
inaccuracies nor for any loss, harm or injury that
comes about from following instructions or advice
in this book.

contents

introduction

Whether decorative or practical, traditional or contemporary, cushions are the perfect finishing touch to an interior. They come in all shapes and sizes and can be used in a room to add a feeling of ease or an air of luxury. There is an abundance of beautiful fabrics that can be made into cushions. Whatever your preferred style, from plain piped cushions and scatter (throw) cushions to fringed or beaded, there are ideas to suit all tastes.

Cushions are the easiest item of soft furnishing to make. The complete novice can tackle the simpler projects shown here, and the clear and concise techniques section at the end of the book will guide you through all the necessary cushion-making skills. You can add a touch of individuality with unusual trimmings, creating endless variations on the basic scatter cushion. It is not only the edges of the cushions that can be decorative; the large area on the front of the cushion cover is an ideal opportunity for beautiful handiwork. Simple machine-embroidered motifs repeated over the surface often look effective, or a larger design can be embroidered. Fabric crafts such as patchwork and appliqué are also suitable.

The majority of cushions may be square or rectangular, but cushion pads are available in various shapes and sizes, including circles and hearts. You can also make your own pad using foam chips, polyester stuffing or feathers. The most expensive filling is feathers, but it lasts much longer than other types and does not go lumpy or flat.

The styles you can choose include box-style cushions, which are similar to scatter cushions but have a gusset running around the edge. Feather-filled, box-style cushion pads are available, but you can also use a specially cut piece of foam. These cushions are ideal for softening a wicker chair or wooden bench, or they can be made in extra-large sizes for window seating. Bolster cushions add an elegant touch, tucked into the arm of a sofa or used as a day pillow on a couch. Formal bolster cushion covers have a classic piped edge and covered buttons or luxurious tassels at each end. With these myriad styles, you will discover that cushions are one of the most versatile accessories.

projects

A traditional Oxford cushion has a plain flat flange around the edge of the cushion pad. The flange is a flat fabric border created by cutting the cushion cover larger than you otherwise would and stitching a line around the edge before inserting the pad.

oxford classic

YOU WILL NEED

cushion pad
paper and pencil to make
 a template
fabric
sewing kit
iron
masking tape (optional)

tips

The size of the flange
should be in proportion
to the size of the pad. A
5cm (2in) flange is ideal
for a 40cm (16in) pad.

Give a softer edge to the
cushion by padding the
flange with strips of
wadding (batting).

STEP 1

STEP 2

STEP 4

1 Measure the cushion pad and add the flange width all around. The flange should be approximately one eighth of the cushion width to be in proportion. Draw a paper template adding 1.5cm (⁹⁄₁₆in) seam allowance and cut out a piece of fabric to this size for the front cover. Fold the template in half widthways and cut out one back panel this size. Cut out another back panel 15cm (6in) longer. Press under or pin a 2cm (¾in) hem on each panel where they will overlap. Machine-stitch.

2 With right sides of the fabric together, pin the back panels along the top and bottom edges to the cushion front. Overlap the hems, keeping the larger panel on top. This will form the envelope opening.

3 Stitch the front and back together with a 1cm (½in) seam, reversing the stitching along the side seams where the hems overlap for extra strength when inserting the cushion pad. Trim across the corners to reduce bulk, ensuring that you do not cut through the seam.

4 Turn the cushion cover through to the right side, ease out the corners carefully and press. Pin and tack (baste) around the cover the width of the flange in from the stitched edge. Stitch just inside the tacked line. Use a piece of masking tape to mark the flange width on the needle plate of your sewing machine, if you like, before beginning to stitch. Carefully remove the tacking threads and insert the cushion pad.

An organza Oxford cover, slipped over a satin cushion makes a theatrical combination. In this project the metallic charcoal grey organza over red satin makes a bold statement, but a more subtle effect can be achieved with a paler cover.

organza duo

YOU WILL NEED
cushion pad
fabric A (satin)
sewing kit
iron
press fasteners
fabric B (metallic
  organza)

tip
When choosing the
fabrics, hold the organza
over the satin to see how
the colours affect one
another when they are
combined.

STEP 1

STEP 3

STEP 4

1 For the front, measure the cushion pad and add 4cm (1½in) all around, then cut out a square of satin (fabric A) to size. For the back, halve the width, add 3cm (1³⁄₁₆in) and cut two pieces of satin to size. Turn, press and stitch a 1cm (½in) double hem on one long edge of each back piece. Pin and stitch front and back together, right sides facing and back pieces overlapping.

2 Clip the corners and turn right side out. On the back opening, stitch pairs of press fasteners evenly. Insert the pad and close the fasteners.

3 For the cover, cut a square of organza (fabric B) for the front, adding a proportionate amount for the flange, and two pieces for the back allowing for the flange on three sides of each. Turn and press a double 1cm (½in) hem on one long edge of each back piece. Assemble and stitch together as for the satin cover, with a 1.5cm (⁹⁄₁₆in) seam allowance.

4 Trim away the seam allowance to 6mm (¼in) from the stitching, and clip the corners. Turn the cover right side out, and top stitch 6mm (¼in) from the folded edge. On the cushion front, pin a line the width you have allowed for the flange in from the edge all around. Tack (baste), then machine-stitch just inside the line. Remove the tacking.

5 On the opening edges of the cover back, mark and stitch pairs of press fasteners at intervals. Insert the satin cushion and fasten the organza cover.

A mitred border is an attractive way to frame an unusual piece of fabric or an embroidered panel. To plan the mitres, draw a template the exact size of the cushion pad and mark the inset panel. The cushion can have a zipper or an envelope opening.

mitred monochrome

1 To make the mitred frame for the inset panel, cut four strips of fabric A the length of the cushion pad plus 1.5cm (⅝in) seam allowance on all sides. Place two strips right sides together, fold back a corner at 45 degrees and press. Open out again and tack (baste) along the foldline.

2 Machine-stitch the two pieces together along the tacked line, beginning 1.5cm (⅝in) from the inside edge. Trim the seam to 5mm (¼in) and press open. Join the other two strips on to the right-angled piece, one at a time, at 45 degrees in the same way to make a square frame.

3 Press under 1.5cm (⅝in) seam allowance on the inside edge of the frame. Centre the inset panel on the reverse side and pin in place, with right sides together. Slip-tack the panel in position from the right side and remove the pins.

4 Folding back one side at a time, machine-stitch the sides of the inset panel to the mitred border. Stop stitching at the seam of each mitre for a neat finish. Remove the tacking threads and press flat.

5 Make the cushion back, either with an envelope opening or a semi-concealed zipper (see pages 56–57). Attach to the cushion front by placing right sides together, pinning and tacking in place, then machine-stitching. Turn the cover through and insert the cushion pad.

STEP 1

STEP 3

STEP 4

YOU WILL NEED
fabric A, for the mitred
  border and cushion
  back
cushion pad
sewing kit
iron
fabric B, for the centre
  panel
dressweight zipper
  (optional)

tip
Mark the size of the
inset panel in tracing
paper so that you can
centre a motif before
cutting out.

Piping adds a professional finish and emphasizes the shape of the cushion, particularly if the piping contrasts with the colour and/or texture of the fabric used for the main body. Piping cord is available in a range of thicknesses.

perfect piping

YOU WILL NEED

cushion pad
fabric A (cushion)
sewing kit
fabric B (piping)
piping cord
dressweight zipper
   (optional)

tips

Join the ends of the piping in the centre of the bottom edge of the cushion using one of the methods in the techniques section.

Choose the thickness of cord according to the size of the cushion and the effect required.

STEP 2

STEP 3

STEP 4

1 Measure the cushion pad and cut a cushion front to size leaving a 1.5cm (⅝in) seam allowance. Make a cushion back, either with an envelope opening, in which case you need two overlapping pieces of fabric, one 15cm (6in) longer than the other, or alternatively with a semi-concealed zipper inserted behind the piping on the bottom edge (see page 59).

2 Cut the piping cord to the required length so that it fits all the way around the cushion pad. Then cut bias strips wide enough to fold over the piping cord (see page 60) leaving a 1.5cm (⅝in) seam allowance. Join the bias strips together to make one long strip of fabric to cover the cord, as described on page 60. Pin the bias strips around the cord and machine-stitch close to the cord, using a zipper foot attachment.

3 Pin and tack (baste) the piping around the edge of the cushion front with raw edges facing outwards. Snip V-shaped notches into the seam allowance to allow the piping to bend around the corners.

4 If using a zipper, tack it face down on to the seam allowance of the front panel and open it slightly. Then, with right sides facing, pin the front and back covers together. Stitch as close as possible to the piping cord, using a zipper foot attachment. If the fabric is slippery, such as velvet, tack them together first. Trim the corners to reduce the bulk and turn through to the right side. Insert the cushion pad.

To create an unusual layered effect for a standard box cushion, use muslin backed with a more tightly woven fabric, such as calico, to stabilize it. Piping is particularly effective here, where it edges both the top and bottom panels of the cushion.

box basics

1 Measure the cushion pad and cut a top and bottom panel from the backing fabric the size of the pad plus 1.5cm (⁵⁄₁₆in) seam allowance all round. Cut the same from the muslin. With wrong sides together, steam press each muslin piece to each backing piece. Tack (baste) the layers together around the edges to hold in place.

2 Make up the required length of piping (see pages 60–61) to fit around both the top and bottom panels. Pin the piping along the edge of the right side of the covers with seam allowances aligned. Snip into the raw edges of the piping at the corners. Join the ends using one of the methods shown on page 61 and stitch in place using a zipper foot attachment.

3 Cut a gusset to fit around three sides of the cushion pad. Cut an additional piece of gusset for the remaining side, adding 6cm (2½in) seam allowance to the width and 1.5cm (⁵⁄₁₆in) seam allowance to the length of one side. Cut this strip in half lengthways and fit a concealed zipper in the centre of it (see page 58). Now join it together with the first piece of gusset to make a continuous strip.

4 With right sides together, tack the gusset in place between the front and back panels of the cover, ensuring that the zipper falls in the centre of one edge. Stitch close to the piping and turn the cover through, easing the corners out. Insert the cushion pad.

STEP 1

STEP 2

STEP 4

YOU WILL NEED

box cushion pad
backing fabric
sewing kit
muslin (cheesecloth)
iron
contrast fabric for piping
piping cord
dressweight zipper

tips

Before fitting the back cover, snip into the gusset at each corner to ensure that it is absolutely square.

Use a backing fabric in a contrasting colour to the muslin.

This oriental-inspired fabric gives an Eastern feel to a round box cushion. The finished result is one of understated chic, perfectly suited to a minimalistic interior scheme. In this variation the gusset is cut on the bias, emphasizing the cushion's plumpness.

oriental chic

1 Measure across the top of the cushion pad, add 1.5cm (⅝in) seam allowance all round and use a compass to draw a circular template of this size. Cut it out. Pinning the template to the fabric, cut one front and one back cover. Measure the depth of the cushion pad.

2 To make the zipper panel, cut one piece of fabric the depth of the pad plus 6cm (2½in) for seam allowances, and the length of the zipper, plus seam allowances. Cut this strip in half lengthways. Insert a semi-concealed zipper and machine-stitch in place (see pages 56–57).

3 Cut out the rest of the gusset, adding 1.5cm (⅝in) seam allowance all round. With right sides together, stitch one end of the gusset to the zipper panel and press the seams open. Pin in place around the front cover.

4 Pin the other end of the gusset to the zipper panel. Remove several pins and stitch the gusset ends together. Open the zipper. Pin the back cover in place. Stitch the cushion back and front in place. Notch the curves. Turn the cushion cover through and insert the cushion pad.

5 Cover the buttons (see page 55). Mark the centre front and back with pins. Using strong thread and a long needle, thread a button on to one side. Push the needle right through the pad. Thread on the other button at the other side. Fasten off the thread securely.

STEP 2

STEP 3

STEP 4

YOU WILL NEED
sewing kit
round box cushion pad
paper, pencil and
   compass to make a
   template
fabric
dressweight zipper
iron
two self-cover buttons

tips
Box cushions usually
have a zipper opening in
the centre of the gusset.

When adding the
buttons, pull the thread
firmly to make an indent
on the surfaces of the
cushion.

Adding a fringe to a plain round cushion gives a softer edge. Used with a patterned fabric, especially a pretty floral one, it forms a feminine finishing touch that will add interest and colour to any corner of the sitting room or bedroom.

circular fringe

YOU WILL NEED
round cushion pad
paper, pencil and
 compass to make a
 template
fabric
sewing kit
dressweight zipper
fringing or braid

tips
To calculate the length
of fringing on a circular
cushion multiply the
diameter by 3.14.

Zigzag-stitch close to the
stitching to finish raw
edges and trim the
excess fabric.

STEP 1

STEP 2

STEP 4

1 Measure the cushion pad and add 1.5cm (⅝in) seam allowance all round. Using a compass, make a semicircular template to this size. Pin it to folded fabric to cut out the cushion front, then cut out two separate back panels, adding 1.5cm (⅝in) to the straight edges.

2 Insert a zipper using the semi-concealed method (see pages 56–57), positioning it across the widest part of the cushion back. Centre the zipper along the straight edge of one back panel and sew following the instructions in the techniques section.

3 Stitch the zipper from the right side. At the corner, count the number of stitches into the centre and stitch the same number on both sides to make sure they are equal. Pin and stitch the front cover to the back.

4 Turn through to the right side and, beginning in the middle of the bottom edge, pin the fringe or braid around the cushion cover. Tack in place. Trim the ends so that they overlap slightly, then neatly fold under the ends so that they meet, and slip-stitch the join.

5 Oversew or back-stitch the braid to the front of the cover, without catching the underside in the stitching. Match the colour of the thread to the braid, using a slightly darker shade if you can't get an exact match, and use the least conspicuous stitch possible.

A frill can be made from matching fabric for a more restrained look, or from a contrast fabric for more impact. Whatever the choice made, it is an attractive way to trim a cushion. Adding piping where the frill joins the front gives a neat finish.

frilled finish

YOU WILL NEED

cushion pad
fabric
sewing kit
piping cord
contrast fabric for piping
dressweight zipper
   (optional)
iron

tips

To find the length of frill required for a circular cushion, measure around the outside edge of the cushion pad and then double the length.

The width of the frill is normally between 7.5cm (3in) and 10cm (4in). Above all it should look in proportion to the size of the cushion.

STEP 3

STEP 4

STEP 5

1 Measure the cushion pad and cut a cushion front with 1.5cm (⅝in) seam allowance all round. Cut enough piping cord to fit around the cushion and sufficient bias strips to cover it. Then join the strips together to make a continuous length (see page 60). Pin around the cord, tack (baste) and machine-stitch in place. Attach the piping to the front cover and join at the bottom using one of the methods described (see page 61).

2 Cut out a cushion back and add a concealed zipper (see pages 56–59) or make an envelope opening (see page 54) as desired.

3 Measure all around the cushion pad and allow twice this length for the frill. Decide on the width of the frill and cut sufficient strips of fabric twice this width, plus 3cm (1³⁄₁₆in) seam allowance. Join short ends with plain seams to form a loop. Press the seams open and trim to 5mm (¼in).

4 Fold the frill in half widthways, right side out and raw edges aligned. Sew two rows of gathering stitches, using a long machine stitch. Start a new thread at each join rather than stitching all the way around.

5 Fold the frill into four. Mark the cushion cover into quarters. Pin the frill to the cover, aligning the folds and marks, then pull up the gathers evenly. Adjust, allowing slightly more fullness at the corners. Tack in position and stitch.

Bolster cushions make ideal armrests or headrests for a sofa or day bed. This design has smooth ends edged with piping for definition. The muted shades and combination of patterned and plain fabrics makes for an understated, but elegant effect.

effortless elegance

1 Measure the end of the bolster pad and make a paper template adding 1.5cm (⅝in) seam allowance all round. Using fabric A, pin the template in position and cut out two circles of fabric.

2 Measure a length of piping cord to fit around the bolster end. Repeat for the other end of the bolster. Cut bias strips in fabric B to cover the piping (see page 60). With raw edges aligned, pin the piping around the edge of each circle on the right side of the fabric. Tack (baste) in place. Join the ends neatly (see page 61) and stitch on using a zipper foot.

3 Cut out the main panel to fit the bolster pad, measuring the circumference of the pad by the length and adding 1.5cm (⅝in) seam allowance all round, plus the amount needed for your chosen fastener. With right sides together, pin the long edges. Mark the position of the gap for inserting the pad, and stitch from the marked points to the edge of the fabric. Add a zipper, buttons and buttonholes or press studs (see pages 56–59).

4 With right sides together, pin the circular ends to the main panel, lining up the join in the piping with the seam on the main body of the bolster. Stitch in place close to the piping using a zipper foot. Trim any excess material to reduce the bulk. Turn through and insert the cushion pad.

STEP 1

STEP 2

STEP 4

YOU WILL NEED
bolster cushion pad
paper, pencil and
    compass to make a
    template
fabric A (ends)
sewing kit
fabric B (body and
    piping)
piping cord
dressweight zipper,
    buttons or press studs
    (snap fasteners)

tips
When stitching a circle, work at a slow speed and feed the fabric at a slight angle to create a smooth curve.

To calculate the length of piping needed for each end, multiply the diameter of the end by 3.14.

A luxurious velvet bolster looks good on a window seat or a chaise-longue. Use up any remnants of furnishing fabric in this simple patchwork cushion. Trim the gathered ends with self-cover buttons, or add tassels for a more decorative finishing touch.

patchwork bolster

YOU WILL NEED

bolster cushion pad
   45cm (18in) long
pinking shears
velvet fabric in orange,
   dark green, light green
   and lilac (or any
   available remnants)
sewing kit
fading fabric marker
two self-cover buttons
button maker (optional)

tip

A simplified version of this cushion can be made using a single piece of fabric, trimmed with wide ribbon.

STEP 1

STEP 2

STEP 5

1 Measure the circumference of the bolster pad. Using pinking shears, cut one piece of orange velvet 21cm (8½in) wide, two pieces each of light green 7.5cm (3in) wide, dark green 10cm (4in) wide, and lilac 17cm (6⅜in) wide by the circumference measurement plus 3cm (1³⁄₁₆in). Adjust measurements proportionately if the bolster pad is a different size. Pin and machine-stitch the strips together along the longest edges.

2 Fold the patched piece in half widthways, with right sides facing, the seams aligned and the raw edges matching. Pin and machine-stitch the seam to form a tube. Turn the cover right side out.

3 Place the cushion pad inside the cover. Using a double thread, run a gathering thread around each end. Draw up the thread, tuck the raw edges inside and stitch to secure.

4 Make the covered buttons. Using the fabric marker, draw around both of the self-cover buttons on the wrong side of a piece of light green velvet, adding a 6mm (¼in) seam allowance. Cut out the circles of fabric.

5 Cover each button using a button maker, or simply sew a running stitch around the edge of each circle and pull up the thread to gather the fabric. Press the backs of the buttons into place. Stitch a covered button over the gathered edge at each end of the bolster.

A covered button makes an attractive finish to gathered ends on a bolster. In this design, a central panel is edged with a contrasting material. This combination of features gives a sophisticated bolster cushion that adds refinement to any setting.

urban style

1 Measure the length and circumference of the bolster. Cut a central panel half the length by the circumference from fabric A, and two borders a quarter of the length from fabric B, adding 1.5cm (⅝in) seam allowance all round. Right sides together, pin and stitch the borders to the main panel.

2 Using fabric A, make piping to fit around the ends of the bolster (see pages 60–61). Pin and tack (baste) in place with the raw edges aligned.

3 For the gathered ends, cut out two lengths of fabric B, the circumference by the radius, plus 1.5cm (⅝in) seam allowance. Stitch to the main body, catching the piping between. Trim the piping cord flush with the seam.

4 Matching the seams, stitch the side seam, leaving a gap wide enough to insert the bolster pad. Insert a zipper (see pages 56–59), if using. Press the seams open.

5 Stitch two rows of gathering threads around each end of the bolster. Pull up the threads tightly. Holding each end in turn, wrap a strong thread round just below the gathers and fasten securely. Turn right side out.

6 Cover the buttons in fabric A (see page 55). Thread them into the centre of the gathers, at each end of the bolster, then stitch securely in place. Insert the bolster pad and slip stitch the gap closed if there is no zipper.

STEP 2

STEP 5

STEP 6

YOU WILL NEED
bolster cushion pad
fabric A (centre panel,
    piping and buttons)
sewing kit
fabric B (ends)
piping cord
dressweight zipper
    (optional)
iron
two self-cover buttons

tip
Use stronger, more defined contrasting colours to create a more dramatic look.

This pretty cushion cover has an opening on one side fastened with ties. The ties can be narrow or wide, and made with square or angled ends. The cushion pad, covered with a contrasting fabric, is visible, creating an attractive layered effect.

tasteful ties

YOU WILL NEED

cushion pad
fabric A (inner casing)
fabric B (outer casing and ties)
sewing kit
iron
masking tape (optional)

tip

The length of the ties depends on whether you want to tie a bow or a simple knot to finish the cushion, so tie a strip of fabric to decide the ideal length for the effect you want.

STEP 1

STEP 3

STEP 5

1 Measure the pad and make the inner casing from fabric A (see page 54). For the front and back outer casing, add 3cm (1³⁄₁₆in) for seams to the width and 20cm (8in) to the length. Cut two pieces of fabric B to this size. With right sides together, stitch three sides. Trim the seams and the corners.

2 Cut four ties twice the width required, plus a 3cm (1³⁄₁₆in) seam allowance from fabric A. Fold each in half widthways, right sides together. Stitch across the top and down the length. Trim the corners and turn through.

3 Cut 17cm (6³⁄₄in) off the length of the casing from the unstitched end, and reserve for the facing. Turn the cover through to the right side and press. Raw edges together, pin the ties to the top of the cover, securing two to each side and making sure they are evenly spaced and that the ties line up on either side. Tack (baste) them securely in place.

4 Turn under a 5mm (¼in) hem along one edge of the facing and stitch. Match the seams. Right sides together and raw edges aligned, pin the facing to the cover, trapping the ties. Stitch in place 1.5cm (⁹⁄₁₆in) from the edge.

5 Press the seam flat between the facing and the cushion cover, then fold the facing to the inside and press the edge from the reverse side. Stitch around the opening, 4cm (1½in) from the folded edge, to secure the facing. Use the lines on the needle plate or attach a piece of masking tape for accuracy. Press.

A beautifully tailored cushion will transform a hard wooden chair, making it more comfortable and warmer to sit on. Select a fabric to match other soft furnishings already in the room. Add ribbon or fabric ties to hold the pad securely in position.

ribboned seat pad

YOU WILL NEED

paper and pencil to make
  a template
fabric A (pad)
sewing kit
fabric B/ribbon (ties)
blunt tool
iron
wadding (batting)
fading fabric marker

tip

Cut a strip of fabric and tie around the chair back to find the exact length of tie required.

STEP 3

STEP 4

STEP 5

1 Make a paper template of the chair seat, marking the position for the ties. Fold it in half. Place the fold along the centre of the design, if any, on fabric A, open out and pin. Cut out two full-size fabric pieces, adding 1.5cm (⁵⁄₁₆in) seam allowance all round.

2 For fabric ties, cut four strips of fabric B, each 8 x 50cm (3⅛ x 20in). With right sides together, fold each in half lengthways. Stitch down the long side and diagonally across one short end to create a neat end. Trim excess fabric to reduce bulk. Turn through and ease out the point with a blunt tool. Roll the seam between your thumb and finger, then press.

3 With raw edges aligned, pin the ties to the back corners of one cut piece of fabric A, on the right side. Bundle the tie ends in the centre, so that they do not get caught in the seams.

4 Place a second cushion piece on top, with right sides together, then add a piece of wadding (batting) cut to size on top. Pin the layers together then stitch around the edge, leaving a gap at the back to turn through.

5 Notch the outward-facing curves and turn through. Ease out the seams and pin all around. Slip-stitch the gap. Using a slightly longer stitch, top-stitch around the cushion 1.5cm (⁵⁄₁₆in) from the stitched edge. Mark with a fabric marker if you are unsure. Tie the pad in position on the chair back.

Combine blue and white gingham buttons with classic linen dish towels to create a simple but stylish cushion for a kitchen chair. The crisp, fresh linen paired with the gingham checks forms a rustic look perfect for a country kitchen.

country kitchen

1 Measure the cushion pad and make a template, adding 1.5cm (⅝in) seam allowance all round. From one dish towel, cut a back piece to size using the template. Fold the template in half along the longest side and cut a piece for the front, then open it up, fold over one-third, to cut a second piece approximately two-thirds the length of the back. Use the edge of the dish towel for one side of the length – this is where the loops will be attached.

2 Cut a strip of fabric A 55 x 4cm (22 x 1½in). Fold in half widthways and press. Open out and fold the sides into the centre, press, then fold in half. Sew along each side, then cut the strip into five 11cm (4⅜in) lengths.

3 Fold each length in half to make a loop, and press. Position the loops along the long edge of the larger front piece, on the wrong side. Tack (baste) in place and then stitch along the hem line.

4 Place the piece with the loops on top of the back piece, with right sides facing, then place the smaller front piece on top. Tack and machine stitch around the edge with a 1cm (½in) seam. Snip the corners, turn right side out and press. Remove the tacking.

5 Cover the buttons with fabric B (see page 55). Sew the buttons in place to match the loops. Insert the cushion pad and fasten the loops.

STEP 2

STEP 3

STEP 5

YOU WILL NEED

cushion pad (smaller than width of dish towels)
paper and pencil to make a template
two linen dish towels
sewing kit
fabric A (button loops)
iron
fabric B (buttons)
five self-cover buttons

tip

Dish towels come in various colours. Pick a shade to suit the colour scheme and select co-ordinating fabrics for buttons and loops.

A neutral colour scheme combined with natural fabrics creates a simple yet sophisticated interior decor. The relaxed atmosphere is enhanced with warm tones suggesting comfort and ease. Looped buttons add a decorative finish to an understated cushion.

natural heaven

YOU WILL NEED

cushion pad
linen fabric
sewing kit
iron
safety pin
8–10 small buttons

tips

To ring the changes, add a splash of colour to a neutral scheme with vibrant shades of blue, red, orange or purple.

Make the button loops out of off-white cord for a simple but elegant alternative.

STEP 1

STEP 4

STEP 5

1 Measure the width and length of the cushion pad. Double the length and add 10cm (4in) for the flap opening, plus 3cm (1³⁄₁₆in) seam allowance all round. Cut the fabric to size, turn back the hems on the short ends and press. Fold the length of fabric as shown, with right sides together, overlapping the ends.

2 Cut a second strip of fabric 7.5cm (3in) wide by the depth of the cushion, plus seam allowance, as an interface.

3 To make the button loops, cut a length of fabric about 2.5cm (1in) wide on the crossgrain. With right sides together, pin, tack (baste) and machine-stitch the fabric. Trim the excess fabric close to the stitching and, using a small safety pin, turn the piping through to the right side. Press flat.

4 Cut a sufficient quantity of loops to a length of about 7.5cm (3in). Pin and tack them in place along the hem of the overlapping edge of the fabric.

5 Pin, tack and machine-stitch the interfacing strip for the opening on the edge with the loops.

6 Now machine-stitch a seam all round the cushion. Turn right side out and press. Mark the positions of the buttons with pins and hand sew in place. Insert the cushion pad and close the loops over the buttons.

A monogrammed lace cushion makes a perfect gift for a loved one. Scraps of pretty white lace combined with delicate pearl beads on a heavily textured linen fabric make a marvellously muted cushion, equally at home on a bed or an armchair.

lace and linen

YOU WILL NEED

paper and pencil to make
   a template
two 22cm (8¾in)
   squares of heavyweight
   linen fabric
fading fabric marker
scraps of white lace
anti-fraying solution
sewing kit
wadding (batting)
90cm (36in) narrow
   white lace edging
beading needle
tiny pearl beads

STEP 2

STEP 3

STEP 5

1 Draw a large capital letter, or motif, about 12cm (4½in) high, on paper and cut out to make a template. Transfer to the right side of one of the linen squares using a fading fabric marker. Cut out lace motifs, including scrolls and flowers, that will fit the shape of the chosen initial or design.

2 Treat the edges of the cut lace with anti-fraying solution. Leave to dry. Arrange the lace motifs on the fabric and tack (baste) in place.

3 Using white sewing thread, stitch the lace motifs in place with very small, almost invisible, stab stitches (see page 53).

4 With wrong sides facing, hand- or machine-stitch the two squares of linen together, 3cm (1³⁄₁₆in) from the edge, leaving a 5cm (2in) gap along one side. Pull away threads for 2cm (¾in) to create a fringe around the edges. Fill the cushion with wadding. Slip-stitch the gap closed with neutral coloured thread.

5 Stitch the narrow lace edging along the stitch line, to cover the stitching and create a decorative border.

6 Using a beading needle, stitch tiny pearl beads to the centre of any flower-shaped motifs. Stitch a daisy-shaped motif or similar shape to each corner of the cushion as a final embellishment.

A collection of colourful brocade ribbons stitched on to a ticking background make a pretty vintage-style cushion. Mix ribbons with strips of fabric for an inexpensive but stunning cushion cover and complete the period effect with a braid border.

vintage style

1 Measure the pad and cut the ticking 5cm (2in) larger all round. Take the lengths of ribbon or fabric strips and cut them in equal lengths approximately to the width of the ticking. Arrange them alongside each other, varying the colours and widths, to make a pleasing design. Any raw edges of fabric strips should be covered with ribbon.

2 Starting from the right-hand side, machine-stitch the fabric strips and wider ribbons on to the ticking with a close zigzag stitch. Follow the stripes on the ticking to keep the ribbons in a straight line. Add the narrow ribbons, stitching them on top of the previous layer.

3 Measure the finished size of ribbon appliqué 2.5cm (1in) larger than the cushion pad and mark a line with a fading fabric marker. Trim to size.

4 Cut two pieces of backing fabric to make an envelope opening. Stitch a narrow double hem along one edge of each square for the back opening. Right sides facing, pin one side to each short edge of the ribbon appliqué with trimmed edges facing inwards. Machine-stitch all round. Turn the cushion-cover right side out, easing out the corners.

5 Starting at one corner, stitch the braid all round the cushion, using slip stitch. Gather the braid slightly at the corners. Conceal the join in the ends at the final corner. Insert the cushion pad.

STEP 2

STEP 3

STEP 5

YOU WILL NEED
cushion pad
ticking
assorted lengths of
   ribbon or strips of
   fabric, in different
   widths
sewing kit
fading fabric marker
ruler
backing fabric
decorative braid long
   enough to fit all round
   the cushion, plus 10cm
   (4in) extra

tip
Always stitch from the
top down to avoid
puckering the ribbons.

Bands of satin, velvet and taffeta ribbon falling diagonally across this silk cushion create a symphony of rich textures. Though all the tones are similar, light plays on the ribbons in different ways with dramatically contrasting effects.

ribbon stripe

YOU WILL NEED
cushion pad
fabric A (silk)
sewing kit
selection of ribbons
stranded embroidery
  thread (floss)
fabric B (velvet)
piping cord
dressweight zipper

tip
Fold silk backing fabric diagonally through the centre and press. Use this line as a guide for arranging the ribbons.

STEP 1

STEP 2

STEP 4

1 For the front, measure the cushion pad and add 2.5cm (1in) all round, then cut out a piece of fabric A to size. Arrange lengths of ribbon diagonally across the fabric and pin in place. When satisfied with the design, tack (baste) the ribbons to the front of the cushion.

2 Using stranded embroidery thread in a range of complementary colours, work rows of feather stitch to join the edges of the ribbons, varying the direction of the stitches (see page 53).

3 Using fabric B cut 4cm (1½in) wide bias strips and join together to create a bias binding. Pin round the piping cord and machine-stitch in place using a zipper foot. Pin round the cushion front with the raw edges matching. Clip the seam allowance at the corners. Tack, then machine-stitch close to the cord using the zipper foot.

4 Trim the cord so the ends butt and lap one end of the casing over the other, turning under the edges. Pin and machine-stitch. Slip-stitch the edge.

5 For the back, cut two pieces of fabric A the length of the pad by half the width, adding 4cm (1½in) all around. With right sides together, match the two long edges and fit a semi-concealed zipper (see pages 56–57). With right sides together, pin and machine-stitch the front and back together following the piping. Clip the corners, turn through and insert the pad.

A collection of luxurious fabric remnants and sparkling trimmings can be transformed into a sumptuous patchwork cushion that will grace any room. Edged with a beaded fringe, this extravagant cushion cover is perfect for a lavish boudoir.

fringed velvet

YOU WILL NEED

cushion pad
velvet fabric (cushion
   back)
sewing kit
dressweight zipper
card and pencil to make
   a template
squares of red, green and
   grey velvet (cushion
   front)
pinking shears
iron
beaded fringing

tip

Scour furnishing-fabric departments of large stores and small haberdashers for beautiful fabric remnants and trimmings.

STEP 1

STEP 2

STEP 5

1 For the cushion back, cut one piece of velvet the width of the pad by two-thirds the length and a second piece the width of the pad by one-third the length, plus 1.5cm (⅝in) seam allowance all round. Join the pieces, inserting a concealed zipper in the centre of the seam (see page 58).

2 Make a triangular card template. Cut out a triangle from red velvet and one from grey velvet, using pinking shears. Then turn the template over and cut out another triangle of each colour. Cut out two green velvet triangles, then turn the template over and cut two more. Pin a green and a red triangle, right sides together, along the diagonal edges. Machine stitch with a 1.5cm (⅝in) seam and repeat for the other pairs of triangles.

3 Pin two rectangles, right sides facing, along their longest edges, matching diagonal seams. Machine-stitch with a 1.5 cm (⅝in) seam. Pin the two halves of the front together, matching the centre seams, and machine-stitch.

4 Press the seams open, and trim down to reduce the bulk. Lightly press the seams on the right side of the fabric, using a cool iron.

5 Measure and cut two lengths of fringing, and pin to the short edges of the cushion front. Machine-stitch in place, using a zipper foot. With the zipper open and right sides facing, pin and machine-stitch the front and back together. Trim the corners and turn right side out. Insert the pad.

The plainest cushion can be dramatically transformed with a beadwork edging. Beads of different weights and sizes give varying effects: small beads make a beautiful delicate fringe, while large glass beads give a much bolder look.

bohemian beads

YOU WILL NEED
cushion pad
striped fabric
sewing kit
iron
fading fabric marker
graph paper and pencil
small glass beads
7mm (¼in) disc-shaped
  beads

tip
Select beads either to
contrast boldly or blend
subtly with the fabric.

STEP 3

STEP 4

STEP 5

1 Measure the cushion pad and, to make the front cover, cut a piece of fabric the size of the cushion pad plus 2cm (¾in) on the width and 20cm (8in) on the length. For the back, cut two pieces the same width as the front and two-thirds the length. Press under a double hem on the short back opening edges and machine-stitch.

2 With right sides facing and stitched edges overlapping, pin and stitch two lengthways seams.

3 Turn right side out and press. Mark a line 10cm (4in) from the raw edges on both sides and topstitch. Gently pull away the fabric close to the stitching. Starting from the outer edges, separate and remove threads up to the stitched line creating a fringe.

4 Mark the length of fringe on graph paper. Cut thread four times this length and double through the needle. Insert the needle at the inner edge of the first stripe of the fabric and secure with a knot.

5 Mix a few small beads with the larger disc-shaped ones in the chosen colour scheme. Thread on 9.5cm (3¾in) of beads, using graph paper as a guide. Thread on a disc-shaped and a small bead. Pass the needle up the strand and make another finishing stitch. Pull gently on the strand to straighten out kinks. Trim the thread. Repeat with the other stripes.

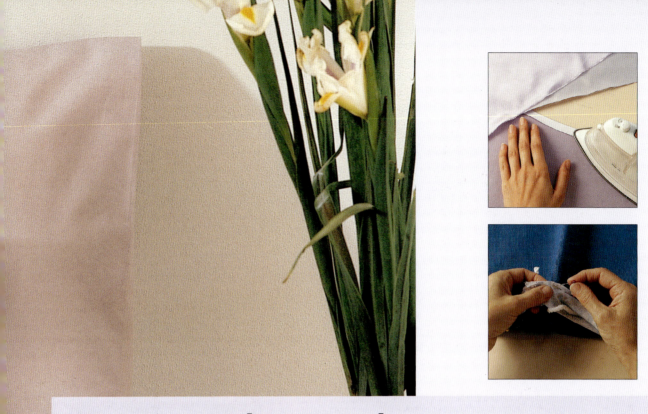

techniques

fabric grain

The grain of a fabric means the way that the threads are arranged. This affects how a fabric hangs and drapes. The grain should always be straight when you cut the fabric; if it is off-grain it needs to be straightened in order to prevent costly mistakes.

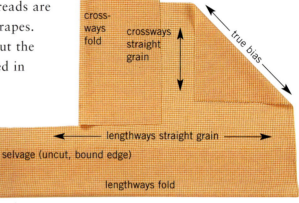

ABOVE: It is important to become familiar with the terms that describe the sections and make-up of fabric.

STEP 1

FABRIC COMPOSITION

In woven fabrics, there are three types of grain. The lengthways straight grain, the long threads that run parallel to the selvage; the crossways straight grain, the threads that run perpendicular to the selvage; and the true bias grain, running on the diagonal.

STEP 2

CUTTING ALONG THE GRAIN

If the fabric has an obvious pattern, such as a check, it can be cut along the grain to ensure it is straight. Otherwise, you will have to tear or cut along a thread to ensure a straight line. To do this, look at the weave and snip into the selvage next to where the first thread goes straight across. Pull one of the crossways threads until the fabric gathers (see step 1). Ease the gathers gently along the thread, then cut carefully through the width along this line (see step 2).

STEP 3

STRAIGHTENING THE GRAIN

Off-grain fabric can result in cushions that are not square. To check whether the fabric is straight, straighten the ends, either by tearing the fabric or by pulling a thread, then fold it in half lengthways with the selvages together to see if the crossways ends meet squarely. If the corners don't match, the grain must be straightened before the fabric is cut.

If the fabric is slightly off-grain it can be steam-pressed back into shape, but if it is severely mis-shapen it must be pulled back into shape. To do this, hold the fabric firmly on each side of the corner and pull apart (see step 3). Move down each side, pulling firmly. Fold in half lengthways, right sides together, and pin the raw edges together. Place pins into the ironing board every 13cm (5in) along the selvage. Press the fabric from the selvage into the fold until the weave is totally straight, but avoid pressing into the fold. Leave to cool before removing the pins.

the sewing kit

You will probably have much of this equipment already in your sewing box. If not, it is worth investing in these basic items to give your cushions a quality finish. Always check that the scissors you use for cutting fabric are perfectly sharp.

1 Sewing machine with foot pedal Any ordinary domestic sewing machine is suitable.

2 Hand-sewing needles 'Sharps' (medium-length, all-purpose needles) are used for general hand sewing. For fine hand sewing, use the shorter, round-eyed 'betweens'. Needles are numbered from 1–10, with 10 being the finest.

3 Sewing threads For best results, choose a type of thread that matches the fibre content of the fabric. Use a shade of thread that matches the fabric. If there is no exact match go one shade darker. Use strong thread for making durable cushion covers, especially if they are to be used regularly. Tacking (basting) thread is cheaper and poorer-quality. Use strong buttonhole twist or linen thread for buttonholes.

4 Scissors You will need a large pair of drop-handle (bent-handle) scissors for cutting out fabric, a medium pair for trimming seams or cutting small pieces of fabric, and a small pair of sharp, pointed embroidery scissors for cutting threads and snipping into curves. Never cut paper with sewing scissors as it dulls the blades.

5 Dressmaker's pins Use normal household pins for most sewing, and lace pins for delicate fabrics. Glass-headed pins are easy to see.

6 Pin cushion Useful for holding pins and needles as you work.

7 Seam ripper A small cutting tool for undoing machine-stitching mistakes quickly. Also useful for cutting buttonholes.

8 Tape measure Select a 150cm (60in) tape with metal tips in a material such as fibreglass that will not stretch. A small metal ruler with an adjustable guide is useful when measuring for buttonholes.

9 Tailor's chalk Used to mark fabric. Keep the edge sharp by shaving it with medium scissors. Test on the right side of the fabric to ensure it will brush off easily.

10 Fabric markers A pencil is suitable for marking most hard-surfaced fabrics and can be brushed off with a stiff brush. A vanishing-ink pen will wash out in water or fade.

making seams

Various seams may be used in different cushion projects, depending on whether the finished item needs to be strong enough to withstand frequent washing or whether it is to be purely decorative. The basic seam used for most cushion projects is a flat seam. An alternative to this is the French seam, which is used for sheer or delicate fabrics. This strengthens the fabric by stitching a double seam.

RIGHT: A flat seam is suitable for a durable fabric and is strong enough to withstand frequent washing.

tip
Seams enclosed within a cushion cover don't have to be finished with an edging stitch, but they should be trimmed carefully, and curves notched, to achieve a neat line when the cover is turned through.

FLAT SEAMS
With right sides together, machine-stitch a seam about 1.5cm (⅝in) from the edge. Trim down if required and press the seam open. Finish the edges with zigzag stitch to prevent fraying.

FRENCH SEAMS
On lightweight or sheer fabrics, a French seam is needed to create a strong join that will not fray. Unlike other seams, a French seam is made by starting with the wrong sides of the fabric together. On very fine fabrics the finished seam can be narrower than given here.

1 Machine-stitch the wrong sides of the fabric together, using 9mm (⅜in) from the seam allowance. Trim this seam to 4mm (³⁄₁₆in).

2 Press the seam open. This makes it easier to get the next fold exactly on the edge of the fabric.

3 Fold the fabric over, with right sides together, enclosing the raw edges. Press the fabric again. Pin the second seam along the seam line 5mm (¼in) from the edge and stitch. Press the seam so it is flat.

STEP 1

STEP 2

STEP 3

hand stitching

The majority of cushions are stitched by machine, but there may be a need for some temporary or permanent hand stitching as well. Temporary stitches, such as tacking (basting), are used to hold fabric in position before stitching and are usually removed later. Permanent stitches include slip-stitch (often used to close a gap), running stitch (mainly used for gathers), back-stitch (for awkward seams) and stab-stitch (for appliqué).

1 TACKING (BASTING)
Work small, even stitches along seams to secure before stitching permanently. Longer, uneven stitches are used to stitch substantial distances.

2 RUNNING STITCH
Several stitches are 'run' on the needle at once, keeping the spaces and stitches the same size. It is used for awkward seams and for gathering, with the thread end left loose for pulling up.

3 SLIP-STITCH
Take a small stitch through the top layer and another through the fabric beneath. Keep the stitches even and the thread straight. Pull the thread taut without causing the fabric to pucker.

4 SLIP-TACKING (BASTING)
These are worked from the right side of the fabric when joining two pieces of fabric.

5 BACK-STITCH
For this strong stitch, take a small stitch back to meet the previous stitch, then bring the needle out the same distance in front.

1

2

3

4

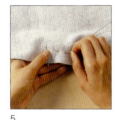
5

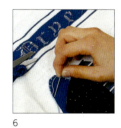
6

6 STAB-STITCH
This is useful for adding appliqué designs. Bring the needle up through the fabric and down again very close to catch a small amount of material.

7 FEATHER STITCH
This is worked from top to bottom as a series of alternate slanting stitches. The thread lies under the needle to form the characteristic loops.

7

envelope openings

An envelope (overlap) opening is a discreet and easy-to-make cushion-cover opening that makes a practical alternative to a zipper. It is made by cutting one piece of fabric for the back substantially longer than the other, forming an overlap. If the two envelope hems overlap by less than 10cm (4in), a fastening, such as buttons, press fasteners or velcro, will be needed to hold the edges together so that the cushion does not gape open.

STEP 1

STEP 2

STEP 3

RIGHT: Envelope openings are an easy-to-make alternative to inserting zippers and a cushion cover with this type of opening makes a good first project for a beginner.

tip Reverse stitch along the side seams, where the hems overlap, for extra strength when inserting or removing the cushion pad.

MAKING AN ENVELOPE OPENING

1 Draw a paper template the same size as the cushion pad. Cut out a full-size piece of fabric for the front cover, adding 1.5cm (⅝in) seam allowance all round. Now cut the template in half widthways. For the cushion back, cut out one panel this size and a second panel about 15cm (6in) longer, adding 1.5cm (⅝in) seam allowance all round. Press under a 2cm (¾in) hem on each panel at the edge, where they will overlap, and machine-stitch.

2 Place the front cover right side up. Pin the back panels to the front along the top and bottom edges with right sides together. Overlap the hems, keeping the larger panel on top, and pin in place. Tack (baste) all round the edges.

3 Machine-stitch the front and back together using a 1.5cm (⅝in) seam allowance. Finish the raw edges with a zigzag stitch. Remove the tacking. Trim across the corners and turn through. Use a blunt tool to ease out the corners to a point. If the overlap is less than 10cm (4in), add fastenings along the opening. Insert the cushion pad.

button closures

This traditional fastening can be decorative or purely functional. If used on the back of a cushion cover, buttons can be quite plain, whereas if used on an envelope opening on the front of the cushion, they will become a feature. Buttons covered in either a matching or contrast fabric give a project a very professional finish. The buttons can be secured either with a buttonhole or a loop made out of fabric or cord.

COVERING A BUTTON

1 Trace or cut the appropriate size circle template from the back of the button kit packet. Cut the required number of circles, 5–7mm (¼in) larger than the buttons, out of the chosen fabric. If the fabric has a pattern, check that it is centred before cutting out the circles.

2 Tie a knot in the end of the thread. Sew a line of running stitches around the edges of the fabric circle, leaving a long tail of thread. Hold the button in the centre of the circle and pull the thread up tightly, so that the fabric gathers.

3 Even out the gathers and tie off. Fit the back of the button over the shank and press firmly into position.

tip
Self-covering button 'blanks' are available in a range of sizes. Metal blanks are only suitable for decorative cushions that will be dry cleaned. Use plastic button blanks if the item is intended to be washed. The method described above can be used with either type of button blank.

LEFT: The direction of the buttonhole depends on where any strain will be applied. The button should pull to one end in the direction of the strain. If the buttonhole is stitched in the wrong direction, it could open up and the button may pop out.

tip
Match the buttonhole thread to the fabric of the cushion cover rather than the button.

STEP 1

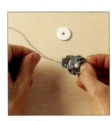

STEP 2

STEP 3

zippers

A zipper is a practical fastener for a cushion cover. Depending on the shape and size of the cushion, it can be placed in a seam, part way down the back, or in the centre of the back. Concealing a zipper in a seam makes sense, but is only suitable if the seam is straight. Zippers are best placed along the bottom edge of a square cushion, or in a side seam on a rectangular cushion. Use a strong dressweight zipper that matches the fabric colour; if it's impossible to get an exact match, a darker shade will be less visible than a lighter one. If fitted well, a zipper will not be very noticeable.

RIGHT: Zippers come in an endless range of colours and sizes. It should be possible to find a close colour match for the cushion fabric you are working with. Select the appropriate size for the cushion project.

SEMI-CONCEALED ZIPPER

This is the simplest way to fit a zipper and it is advisable to master this method before tackling either of the other techniques for fitting zippers. It is called 'semi-concealed' because the teeth are just visible between the folds of fabric. It can be used to insert a zipper in a seam or along the gusset of a box-style cushion.

1 Position the zipper near the edge of the fabric centred on the length and mark each end of the teeth with a pin. Stitch the seam from the pin to the edge of the fabric at both ends.

2 Sew a row of small, even tacking (basting) stitches between the stitched seams. Press the seam open and place the cushion cover right side down on a flat surface.

3 Open the zipper fully and place it right side down with the teeth along one edge of the tacked seam. Pin to the fabric 3mm (⅛in) from the outside edge of the teeth.

STEP 1

STEP 2

STEP 3

4 Tack in place and remove the pins. Close the zipper, then pin and tack the second side in the same way. Mark each end of the zipper teeth with tacking stitches. Fit the zipper foot in the sewing machine. Working from the right side, stitch just outside the tacking thread line. Begin part way down one side of the zipper.

5 When you come to the end of the zipper teeth, where you marked with tacking stitches, leave the needle in the fabric and rotate by 90 degrees, ready to stitch across the end of the zipper. Stitch slowly to the centre of the zipper, then count the number of stitches into the centre of the zipper and stitch the same number out to the other side.

6 Continue stitching down the other side and across the end. Remove the tacking thread from around the stitching, then snip and pull the tacking thread from the centre of the seam.

tip
Use a dressweight zipper 5–10cm (2–4in) shorter than the side seam it is going to fit into.

ABOVE: Fitted well, a semi-concealed zipper will be inconspicuous, but not totally invisible.

STEP 4

STEP 5

STEP 6

STEP 1

STEP 2

STEP 3

STEP 4

ABOVE: A concealed zipper is often used when there is fringing, braid or tassels attached to the edges of the cushion.

CONCEALED ZIPPER

If a square or rectangular cushion has any attachments such as tassels, braid or fringing that could get caught in the zipper teeth, it is better to fit the zipper in the middle of the back panel of the cushion, away from the tassels or fringing. The following instructions show a simple way to fit a concealed zipper. The zipper is inserted to one side of the seam so that the teeth are covered with fabric.

1 Place the pattern pieces right sides together and position the zipper along the seam it will fit into. Mark the ends of the zipper teeth with pins. Stitch the seams from the pins to the outside edge of the fabric at both ends.

2 Sew a row of small, even tacking (basting) stitches between the stitched seams. Press the seam open. Pin the opened zipper with the teeth in the centre of the fabric fold. Tack 3mm (⅛in) from the teeth.

3 Close the zipper and tack the other side to match. Fit the zipper foot in the machine.

4 On the right side of the fabric, stitch close to the fold on the lower edge and just outside the tacks on the upper side. Remove the tacks.

FITTING A ZIPPER BEHIND PIPING

When fitting a zipper on a cushion that is edged with piping, the zipper can be tucked in behind the piping, making it almost invisible. It takes a little extra care and attention, but is worth the trouble to achieve a truly professional finish.

1 Make the piping and tack (baste) on to the front panel of the cushion. Centre the zipper, face down, along the seam allowance of the bottom edge, if square, or the side, if the cushion is rectangular. Pin and tack in place, tacking across the ends of the zipper teeth.

2 Fit the zipper foot in the sewing machine. Open the zipper and stitch 3mm (⅛in) away from the zipper teeth. Stitch halfway down one side of the zipper.

3 Lift the presser foot and close the zipper, easing the slider under the foot. Stitch the rest of the way down the zipper.

4 Pin and tack the other side of the zipper to the back of the cover. Stitch 3mm (⅛in) away from the teeth, lowering the slider as before.

5 Stitch the seams at either end of the zipper with the same number of stitches to each side.

BELOW: The zipper fits in neatly behind the piping on the bottom edge of the cushion and is totally invisible when the cushion is arranged on a chair.

STEP 1

STEP 2

STEP 3

STEP 4

STEP 5

piping

A piped edging adds elegance to a cushion, giving it a top-quality finish and elevating it from everyday status to something quite striking. It is most often used on a cushion to define and accentuate the shape. The plain white piping cord used is available in various widths, ready to be covered with co-ordinating or contrast fabric to the main body of the cover, depending on the cushion design. Patterned fabrics look particularly effective when one of the colours is picked out in the piping. The covered piping cord is sandwiched between the fabric layers and stitched into the seam to give a neat finish.

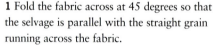

ABOVE: Piping cord comes in a range of thicknesses. Heavier fabrics on large cushions can take thicker cords, but finer fabrics look best with narrower cords.

MAKING BIAS STRIPS

The strips of fabric used to cover the piping cord are usually cut on the bias, but checked and striped fabrics are often cut on the straight grain to ensure that the pattern matches exactly. This method of making bias strips is suitable for most cushions that require fairly small strips.

1 Fold the fabric across at 45 degrees so that the selvage is parallel with the straight grain running across the fabric.

2 Press the diagonal line, then open it out. Cut along this line. Decide on the width and mark lines across the fabric, using a pencil and ruler. Cut sufficient strips to complete the project.

3 Join the strips by overlapping the ends at 45 degrees. Pin, then stitch together.

4 Press open and trim off the triangles. Join sufficient strips together in the same way. Steam-press to remove any excess stretch.

STEP 2

STEP 3

STEP 4

Piped edging not only forms a decorative finishing touch to a cushion, but it also defines the shape, giving it more structure.

STEP 2

STEP 3

STEP 4

APPLYING PIPING

The strips of fabric are wrapped around the piping cord and enclosed within the seams.

1 Cut strips of fabric wide enough to fit around the piping cord, leaving the required seam allowance flat. Fold the strips over the piping cord and pin in place.

2 Fit a zipper foot to the sewing machine. Stitch as close to the piping cord as possible, removing the pins as you go. You can move the needle across slightly so that it stitches at the very edge of the zipper foot.

3 Pin and tack (baste) the piping to the edge of the main fabric. If the bias strips were cut to the correct width, the seam lines will be accurate.

4 Place the second layer of fabric on top and pin. Tack if the fabric is slippery. Stitch as close as possible to the piping cord, moving the needle over if required.

JOINING PIPING

Piping cord is quite bulky and must be trimmed where the ends join together. The piping can simply be 'run off' the edge of the fabric where a join will be inconspicuous. Alternatively, the bias strips can be seamed and the cord trimmed so that the join is not noticeable.

Simple join 1 This is ideal if the join is at the base of a cushion. Open out the ends of the piping and trim the cord so that it meets neatly. Fold the bias strip back over the cord and pin flat on to the seam allowance. Overlap the other end and tack (baste) along the edge of the cord.

Seamed join 1 Open out the ends of the piping strips and pin together with a diagonal seam so that it fits the gap. Stitch the seam and trim to 5mm (³⁄₁₆in). Press open.

2 Overlap the piping cord and trim the ends to different lengths. Refold the binding and tack in place, forming a continuous piece of piping.

STEP 1

STEP 1

STEP 2

flange edges

A flange gives a cushion a more dramatic look by making it appear much larger than it actually is. The flange can be a contrasting fabric, or the same fabric as the main part of the cushion. The width should be in proportion to the size of the cushion and can be variable, as long as the border maintains its tension around the corners. Start by cutting a front cushion panel, and make a back panel with either an envelope or zipper opening.

RIGHT: A flange can be trimmed with cord, ribbon, beads or buttons to exaggerate it and enhance its decorative effect. These toning colours give a subtle definition.

MAKING A FLANGE

1 Tack (baste) the front and back panels with wrong sides together. Cut eight strips of fabric each 7.5cm (3in) wide and 15cm (6in) longer than each cushion edge. Fold back one corner of each strip until the raw edges align. Trim each on the diagonal.

2 Pin the corners right sides together and stitch, stopping 1.5cm (⅝in) away from the inside edge. Make two square flange panels in this way and press the corner seams flat.

3 Pin the two flange panels right sides together. Machine-stitch round the outside edge. Clip the corners and trim the seams to reduce bulk.

4 Turn right side out. Ease out the corners and press. Tuck the tacked cushion panels inside the flange, then pin and machine-stitch.

tip
A ratio of approximately 1 to 8 is a good proportion for the flange, so a 5cm (2in) flange would be ideal for a 40cm (16in) cushion pad.

STEP 1

STEP 3

STEP 4

cushion pads

For an unusually shaped or particularly large cushion, it may be necessary to make the pad as well as the cover. This is not a difficult task and can open up a whole world of possibilities so long as the shape is reasonably simple. The pad can be stuffed with feathers, polyester stuffing or foam chips. Feathers are the most expensive choice, but they last much longer than other types of stuffing and do not tend to go lumpy or flat.

MAKING A HEART-SHAPED PAD

A heavyweight calico casing should be used for feather cushion pads to help prevent the feathers from escaping through the fabric.

1 Draw the desired cushion shape on paper. In this case it is a heart. Use this as a template to cut out two pieces of calico, including a 1.5cm (⅝in) seam allowance all round. Tack (baste) the two pieces together.

2 Stitch round the edge, leaving a gap along one of the straighter edges. If you are making a heart shape, snip into the 'V' at the top and notch the curves. Turn through and stuff firmly with the chosen filling.

3 Pin the gap closed and machine-stitch or slip-stitch the cushion opening. Now re-use your template to cut the fabric for the cushion cover.

tip

If using feathers, keep them securely inside a bag while making the cushion pad to limit the amount of escaped feathers.

STEP 1

STEP 2

STEP 3

LEFT: Small, shaped cushions add interest rather than comfort to a group of scatter (throw) cushions. Choose any shape you want as long as you can make a template.

index

ACKNOWLEDGEMENTS
All photographs © Anness
Publishing Ltd

Photography: Paul Bricknell
(p9, 13, 15, 16, 18, 21, 23,
24, 28, 31, 33, 45); Mark
Wood and Adrian Taylor
(p11, 27, 34); Graeme Rae
(p37); Polly Wreford (p38
and 41); Lucinda Symonds
(p43); Peter Williams (p47).

Projects: Isobel Stanley:
Organza Duo (p10–11),
Patchwork Bolster
(p26–27), Fringed Velvet
(p44–45), Bohemian Beads
(p46–47; Dorothy Wood:
Oxford Class (p8–9),
Mitred Monochrome
(p12–13), Perfect Piping
(p14–15), Box Basics
(p16–17), Oriental Chic
(p18–19), Circular Fringe
(p20–21), Frilled Finish
(p22–23), Effortless
Elegance (p24–25), Urban
Style (p28–29), Tasteful
Ties (p30–31), Ribboned
Seat Pad (p32–33); Petra
Boase: Country Kitchen
(p34–35), Lace and Linen
(p38–39), Vintage Style
(p40–41); Andrea Spencer:
Natural Heaven (p36–37);
Lisa Brown: Ribbon Stripe
(p42–43).